UNDER THE KEEL

UNDER
THE KEEL
MICHAEL
CRUMMEY

ANANSI

This edition published in 2013 by
House of Anansi Press Inc.
110 Spadina Avenue, Suite 801
Toronto, ON, M5V 2K4
Tel. 416-363-4343
Fax 416-363-1017
www.houseofanansi.com

Distributed in Canada by
HarperCollins Canada Ltd.
1995 Markham Road
Scarborough, ON, M1B 5M8
Toll free tel. 1-800-387-0117

Distributed in the United States by
Publishers Group West
1700 Fourth Street
Berkeley, CA, 94710
Toll free tel. 1-800-788-3123

House of Anansi Press is committed to protecting our natural environment. As part of our efforts, the interior of this book is printed on paper made from second-growth forests and is acid-free.

17 16 15 14 13   1 2 3 4 5

Library and Archives Canada Cataloguing in Publication

Crummey, Michael
Under the keel / Michael Crummey.

Issued also in electronic format.
ISBN 978-1-77089-269-9 (pbk).—ISBN 978-1-77089-347-4 (bound.)

I. Title.

PS8555.R84U63 2013   C811'.54   C2012-906732-6

Library of Congress Control Number: 2012950667

Cover design: Brian Morgan
Text design: Alysia Shewchuk
Typesetting: Lynn Gammie

 Canada Council
for the Arts
Conseil des Arts
du Canada

 ONTARIO ARTS COUNCIL
CONSEIL DES ARTS DE L'ONTARIO

We acknowledge for their financial support of our publishing program the Canada Council for the Arts, the Ontario Arts Council, and the Government of Canada through the Canada Book Fund.

Printed and bound in Canada

Holly Ann

THROUGH A GLASS DARKLY

The Selected	3
Boys	5
Girls	7
The Mucky Ditch	9
Odysseus as a Boy	10
Through a Glass Darkly	11
Cock Tease	12
The Skeptics	14
The Mud Hole	15
Albert	17

UNDER THE KEEL

Dead Crow #2	21
Datsun	22
Tusk	23
Fox on the Funk Islands	25
Minke Whale in Slo-Mo	28
Minke in Slo-Mo, Again	29
Leviathan	30
Suffer the Little Children	31
Judas Rope	32
Fathom	34

DEAD MAN'S POND

Patience 37

Water Mark 39

Confession 45

Small Clothes 47

Women's Work 49

Dead Man's Pond 50

Cause of Death and Remarks 52

Mark Waterman, Lightkeeper (Retired)... 53

Stars on the Water 55

Birding, Cape St. Mary's 57

UNDER SILK

In Transit 61

Hope Chest 63

The Kids Are Alright 69

Getting the Marriage into Bed 70

Pub Crawl in Dublin 72

Grand Canal Hangover 74

Vampires, Etc. 76

Dahlias 77

Under Silk 79

THE LANDING

A Carry-On   83

Off-stage   84

Deadfall   86

The Ganges, at Middle Age   88

The Landing   90

Questions of Travel   92

A Stone   94

A Keepsake   95

Viewfinder   96

Burn Barrel   98

The Stars, After John's Homebrew   100

THROUGH
A GLASS
DARKLY

On a short haul flight to Boston
with *The Selected Paul Durcan,*
Irish lines conjuring the Catholic
girl who taught me to neck—
her mouth a marriage of cigarettes
and Wrigley's spearmint,
my hands two raw cadets
assigned their permanent
station: the blue denim
circling those extravagant hips.

And younger, stalking minnows
in a pond set among spruce
trees beside the Catholic manse;
the handsome Father who
played tennis in white shoes,
who flew his own plane,
and eventually renounced
the priesthood for a woman.

All the way to Logan
International, the twinge
of something left behind
at the airport in Halifax
while waiting for my connection,
a loss I can't coax
clear of faint apprehension.
The stewardess leans in
to offer a tray of snacks,
a small silver crucifix

tick-tocking below her perfect
smile, one immaculate hand
marred by the fleck
of a gold wedding band.

BOYS

Not old enough to pay for our trouble,
or even name it, we wandered the town

after dark like dogs, half-tamed at best.
We set small fires and hurled rocks and pissed

against school doors, nosing the margin
of the disallowed, the out of bounds.

We ranged as far as the train trestle,
sniffing underbrush and the long grass

for anything dead or lost or unusual,
broke into empty buildings for the thrill

of stealing through forbidden spaces,
of standing at darkened windows, invisible

while the innocent traffic drove past.
We perched at the lip of change, we knew it,

though in our eyes time itself stood still,
we couldn't imagine ourselves at thirty

or married or living other places —
what we wanted was to see the world undress,

to lie down naked somewhere dirty
and fuck, to do all the unspeakable

things our green minds could only intuit,
a communal urge we suffered alone.

Half-grown, we were living our life by halves,
our dreams were vacant rooms we didn't own

and roamed in silence, shadows behind dark glass,
our mute hearts a mystery to ourselves.

GIRLS

Their bodies were stripling and sleek
and more or less like our own

but for the one alien nook
that made them partial to skirts

and the Easy-bake oven,
clumsy with a hockey stick—

it was the only explanation
the world offered for their eccentric

habits, their feminine quirks,
and it was too simple and stark

a truth to be refuted:
you stood or sat to take a piss

which was the final word on
how a soul was constituted.

Even the beauties who were rough
and tumble, who were known to pick

a fight and could use their fists
carried that internal question mark,

a riddle we couldn't solve or evade.
They were a fruitless provocation,

a rattling kernel of magic
we pretended did not exist,

ten years old and already afraid
we'd never get far enough

inside that cleft's niggling divide
to understand what makes them tick.

THE MUCKY DITCH

A corrupted brook that filtered through bog
beside the mill, a glittering trough of mine
tailings whose narrow passage halved the town,
its muddy verge and surface iridescent
with arsenic and sulphur and ore slag.

It was a lit cigarette, a tropical plant
in a coniferous landscape, and we spent
hours soaking our shoes in the toxic sog,
floating sticks and seedpods on the current,
mucking bare-handed in the auroral brine.

It was a honeyed channel, an oily serpent
urging against an explicit parental ban—
we suffered their discipline without complaint,
made promises knowing we would renege
for the water's radiance, its poisonous sheen.

ODYSSEUS AS A BOY

He's just tied his sitter to a chair
when the telephone rings in the kitchen—

a call for her, of course, and he flays
at the clumsy knots, red-handed, red-faced,

the teen shouting toward the receiver
to say she's coming and urging him on

in a whisper. He's not quite seven,
precociously horny, and embarrassed

to find himself roped to that mast
on such an oddly public stage,

so confounded he can't find the strand
that would lead him through the maze

contrived at each slender wrist.
The girl's fetching voice in his ear

insistent, pealing like a siren.

Dork-faced in mask and snorkel
I bellied into the swimming hole,
occupied innocent hours with pedestrian

revelations below the surface at the Overfalls,
Vaseline smear cleared from my view,
rock and broken bottles and one drowned shoe

rendered with a pornographer's clarity.
Didn't raise my eyes from the water
till I happened on a bayman's daughter

with her hand down some boy's Speedo—
it was the briefest teenage grope
and she kicked clear when he tried to cop

a feel through her bikini bottoms
but that furtive handjob caught in
my flesh like a hook. Couldn't identify

her face among the faces like blossoms
dotting the surface when I glanced up,
the girl found out and still incognito—

that mystery working its way through
my days even now, a piece of shrapnel
from a conflict so old it's nearly forgotten.

COCK TEASE

She had a raw mouth for twelve,
barely-there breasts and a name that made
her reckless and surly by turns.

She liked to be touched and could see
it might be her undoing, she fended off
advances with a savage fatalism

or shifted just out of reach like a sunbather
avoiding a creeping block of shade.
It was wrong to want the kind of attention

boys were willing to give her
and she circled as close as she could
without brushing against it,

she brushed against it with her eyes
averted before startling away
like something scalded.

I was embarrassed to court
her company but risked the taint
for her reputation's promise,

hand working beneath her cotton shirt,
fingers grazing the surprising length
of a nipple before she bolted,

though never far enough to shut the door
completely. That crude tug of war
was everything on offer between us

and we chafed against each
other with a sour sort
of affection.

Out front of Fong's restaurant he choked down
a lit cigarette for quarters and our juvenile edification,
a dozen gawkers taking in the carny sideshow.

Hard to guess what he wanted enough to swallow
that pinprick of coal, whether the contortion
and coughing were genuine or cheap theatrics

to convince us we'd got value for our silver,
but he managed to win over the vocal skeptics
and we all ponied up our promised share.

Not much older than his teenaged audience,
the shoulder-length hair, the filthy shirt and pants
suggested a Sunday-school Jesus expelled

for soiled fingernails, a junkie's demeanour,
his face tortured and strangely calm as he trawled
through the dirt for coins we tossed from the stair,

jukebox and a pinball game inside the entrance
our only amusement when he was done
and the night limped on in its wounded fashion.

THE MUD HOLE

The water fed down from a dam
below the trestle, a steady fall
of clear and cold, and what the name
referred to or why it stuck was
a mystery, even to our parents.
For most it was just a private spot
for drinking beer and making out
beyond adult interference,
a place we could curse our fool
heads off and make rash promises
during bouts of impossibly
acute and fugitive romance.
The recklessly drunk among us
daredevilled off rock ledges
that penned the swimming hole
on three sides, though only the truly
lunatic made the highest dive
from a column known as Tower Five
that slanted alarmingly away
from the pool's dark eye.
We traded mythic stories of those
who failed to clear the outcrop
lurking underwater at the base
and smashed a head or leg or hip,
though the cautionary gossip
wasn't enough to convince
the crazies to take a pass.
On all sides the rocks were littered
with generations of graffiti,
an incomplete fossil record

of the town's desires and grudges
and youthful indiscretions,
which was one of the reasons
adults kept their distance
once they'd moved on to work
and marriage and kids of their own,
avoiding the constant allusion
to what idiots they were back
in the day, how stupidly happy,
how abrupt and lethal the drop
from Tower Five to the water's black.

ALBERT

My last summer we hung out at Fong's
restaurant, at the penstock or the Mud Hole,
waiting for something to happen,
drove aimlessly through town with Albert

who was seventeen and worked part
time to cover his gas, his hash, his beer.
His girlfriend scooched toward the gear
shift to make room as we climbed in

to troll the quiet streets an hour
with all the car windows down,
the radio high enough we had to shout
to be heard above the incandescent,

sugary marl of the latest hit songs.
The girlfriend was blonde and slender
which was enough to pass for beautiful
in a backwater town that small

and Albert shocked us by dumping her
in August. "She wouldn't even give
me a bit of finger skin," was his rationale
and we didn't ask for more detail,

though I'd never heard the term before
and had to guess at what it meant.
Nothing much happened in those final
weeks, beyond our slow meander

through the streets I was about to leave
for good, almost fourteen and still a virgin—
more profoundly so, it turned out,
than I'd even considered possible.

UNDER
THE KEEL

DEAD CROW #2

Baffed out in the street as if taking a spell
at the tail end of an epic bender,
a wedding guest guttered in his best suit,

comically dishevelled and tucked under
the sidewalk's narrow ledge —
the physical manifestation of an effete

English accent pickled in alcohol,
eyes studying the morning's blue for a star.
Halfways tempted to give it a nudge

to see if the drunken lush might stir,
stopped short by the cadaverous feet,
like two bare twigs of alder,

looking unnaturally naked and exposed.
Glance around a moment as I edge
past, wondering what became of those shoes.

DATSUN

Dumped and torched in the White Hills decades back
and everything remotely organic—
cushions, tires and vinyl, interior fabric—
long ago stripped from the scrawny wreck
by fire, by decay's reckoning *tick tick tick*.
All year it squats there, listing off the track
in the approximate shape of a ransacked
four-door sedan with automatic
transmission, though each season the trick
is less convincing and that rusting lock,
soon enough, will be impossible to pick.

Meantime, the woods improvise a meadow
in its coldframe, seeding the import's hollow
shell with alder, with fern and willow,
all craning their heads out a window
or doors hanging ajar, a wayward crew
on a summer road trip, the Datsun's slow
collapse just countryside they're passing through.

TUSK

They gimped into town
driving geriatric trucks,
circled their rinky-dink
convoy on the softball
field's faded diamond,
a duct-taped carnival
of slapstick clowns,
a clutch of dismal
animal acts.
They were a grim crowd,
setting up in the next
dog-eared company hole
down a dead-end road,
barking at the little fucks
who descended to gawk
inside their mobile
homes, to watch them unload,
then stake and pole
a withered circus tent.

Nosed out the main event
before the show began,
a small, squat elephant
chained in a makeshift
stall behind a trailer,
the behemoth no taller
than myself at ten.
Wary, intelligent
eyes above a single rail,

the absurdly deft
prehensile trunk
climbing shyly
in my direction—
it took all my mettle
to meet the gesture
halfway, to barehand
that whiskered husk,
so alien and animate
my arm reared
back like I'd been shot.

It was missing one
stubby yellow tusk,
a sad asymmetry
that each day afterward
I somehow felt
was more and more my fault.

FOX ON THE FUNK ISLANDS

She drifted down from the Strait on an ice pan
and played havoc with the breeding season,

the only predator within fifty miles—
wandering the well-stocked aisles,

chasing seabirds off their roosts for the tasty
morsel of fresh eggs, gorging on the delicacy,

and she killed a freezer-load of adults as well,
caching the carcasses she was too full

to eat, an ancient northern instinct, a store
against the meagre months of winter.

We gave her no chance on the Funks
after the colony migrated, thinking once

snow settled in on that deserted ground
she would starve to death or drown

in the bottomless cold, too rich
an appetite for an economy so strict,

but she was waiting for us in June
having survived the winter dark alone,

making a long celebratory meal
of anything she could chase down and kill.

The returning birds unsettled, too skittish
to lay or tend their chicks in the nest,

and all summer we set traps, hoping to take
her alive; each time she stole the bait,

leaving some small gift in trade,
a razorbill's head, a puffin's wing laid

beside the trigger inside the useless device
as a thank you or a taunt, and once or twice

a week she hung near the camp to watch us,
her stare calm and intently curious.

We were an inconsequential riddle
on the margins of her concern, an idle

interest indulged at her leisure,
and what she made of us being there

preoccupied our talk as we picked away
at the summer's banding survey,

imagining ourselves in her predicament,
anomalous and intransigent,

wild and sovereign, hopelessly astray—
and we admired the creature, grudgingly.

Shot her our last week out there before the boat
arrived, and we each laid a hand to the ratty coat

as if to apologize for the necessary offence,
a gesture of awkward, amoral reverence.

A dark patch of ocean blisters up near
the gunwale with alien deliberation,

sea-water on the rising surface crackling
and receding like celluloid snared in

a projector's heat before the grappling
hook of the dorsal fin enters the frame,

pinning the shapeless shape to a name,
to identifiable attributes and traits,

the yellow dory jarred by the collision
then rocking back as the minke shears

down and away and disappears
like a drunk driver fleeing a minor

accident through backroads, deserted streets.
Repeat the thirty-second clip a dozen

times for the little mystery's slow-motion
resolve, for that rough kiss so impulsive

and unexpected it leaves the diminutive
wooden boat shaking on the ocean.

MINKE IN SLO-MO, AGAIN

Juvenile humpback out for a joy-ride
according to experts, misidentified
in amateur accounts by ambiguous markers—
the whale's relatively small stature,
the underdeveloped dorsal fin.
Buzzing the yellow dory for kicks,
a lark on a grey morning, the cetacean
version of nicky nicky nine doors,
prank call from a briny phone booth,
strike God's fear into the fool at the oars
and drive like hell, you can almost hear
the tires peal on pavement—oh youth!
your hapless bravado, your lethal pride!
your bottomless well of fart jokes!
On some ocean corner the little punk
has replayed the story of this encounter
a dozen times while bumming smokes,
each rendition veering further from the truth,
if he can scrape up enough change before
nightfall he plans to get good and drunk,
go raise some hell up around Carbonear.

A military bunker submerged in the Hills during the war,
leviathan girth poured a fathom below the standard-
issue camouflage of blueberry scrub and alder,
belly stogged with fuel barrels, munitions, bored
American servicemen evading the merciless weather.

Jimmied by underage drinkers, the graffitied door
lists from iron bolts, yaws wide on a caustic dampness,
daylight washing across a concave ceiling; the floor
strewn with civilian storage, retail shelves and desks
being slowly digested in shadows at the rear.

A fire's remains inside the entrance, broken beer
bottles, a pissy stink of decay in the submarine air—
the docile giant defenceless in shallow water,
suffering the casual abuse of teenage delinquents
with its lumbering grace, its impotent ocean silence.

A snap in the cupboard below the kitchen
sink as we made love down the hall,
a distant alarm that didn't register
properly and was all but forgotten before
we surfaced into the morning's run-of-the-mill;
hours till it crossed my mind again,
poking through rags and cans of cleanser—
the little lamb nailed to its crucifix
in the gloom, wire embedded in fur,
two vermin eyes like polished beads.

Children, there is no measure that sets
good against affliction, the world bleeds
one into the other without weighting a scale
and only a fool reads give and take in
the equation; the fool in me suffering
a twinge of remorse to hear the kill bar
hammer home a second time, the echo
distinct and unmistakeable, that trifling
execution casting its three-ounce shadow
on our own inconsequential pleasure.

JUDAS ROPE

We put the old girl
down and it went badly,
the needle's spike
shredding her gauzy veins,
one and then another,
the rogue anesthetic
a torch to her final
moments, and she
writhed her ugly way
through the bonfire
we made of her exit.

Stumbled on the remains
of a dog shot near the lake
when I was eleven,
skeleton tied to a spruce,
the rope's grey skein
just beginning to fray—
a parable on display,
an Old Testament scene
laid out as if to say
What holds a body
to the world betrays us
in the long run,
though I was too young
or too squeamish
to mark the lesson.

We could barely restrain
the lunging animal,
her canine sum reduced
to ninety pounds of anguish
on stainless steel
before a second
injection cut the line;
the vet was a rookie
from Palestine,
he offered a subtle
bow of apology
as we backed away
from the silver table.

The Judas rope still noosed
in the shade of that tree.

Watch the shoulder's ridge ride
beneath the razored patch of skin
as the dog shifts on his bed,
the wound's black and vermilion
length slipping over bone
like a line across a gunwale
as it rises on an easy swell,
new stitches a row of knots tied
to sound fathoms under the keel.

Two young huskies had him pinned
when the blood-of-a-bitch sharked in
from behind, the primeval hinge
of the creature's jaw pincered
shut before the danger registered
in some ancient recess of my mind
and I started to holler,
wading into the savage roil
to kick the bigger dog clear.

The vet revealed a nickel-
sized puncture below the collar,
using both hands to lift his hide
at the spot where the Shepherd
latched and shook its axe-shaped head,
and I stared into that black well
as if my own animal
features might be reflected there,
heartsick and twisted and feral.

DEAD MAN'S POND

This is my kitchen, mine and Gasker's. Him with the hands on his knees like he's about to help himself to his feet. Even set still he seems on his way to some bit of work or other. But that's only show these days. Can't get out of his own way most of the time, spends his nights turning like a spindle on a lathe, the aches working at him. He got old of a sudden and I never saw it coming.

There's people claim the second sight and I count myself lucky to have the first. Twenty-seven when my sister died. Gasker left with two young ones and I never saw it coming all the same, him proposing. Not the marrying kind was what people said, and me along with them. Aunt Annie set me on Mother's stomach when I was born and said, Put a pair of boots on that one, Sarah, she's ready for the woods.

That one over there is my daughter Patience. First child of my own. I had no time for youngsters in those days and I thought it would be a nice reminder. It's hard to stand in the middle of a room yelling Patience! without feeling like a fool.

It didn't always work. But nothing ever does.

She still got the look of it about her. Like the firmament could fall into the ocean and her with the hands folded in her lap like that, calm as you please.

Don't mind the dress and apron on me, I was never happier than in the backcountry hauling wood or setting snares or picking berries in over the barrens. Can't be at that sort of business now though, Gasker the way he is. And sitting don't bother me like it used to. Had near enough of life to do me, I guess. In my mind I'm still knocking around in the woods most of the time I sit by this window, washing out in the light.

This is the kitchen, like I said. First time I ever set for a photograph. Some American stopping in on the coastal boat. I thought the man was simple is the truth of it, ducking in behind that box of his, waving at us to hold still. If I'd known it would mean being gawked at by you crowd I'd have told him to put the machine away, sit to a cup of tea like a sensible person.

Saved myself all this gabbing.

WATER MARK

Pentecostal Baptism, Catalina ca. 1940

1.

Place the tips of my shoes
at the ocean's lip
so I can hold my Bible
out over the surface
Spirit of God moving on the water
Brother Harold up to his arse
in the shallows
salt riming the nap
of his Sunday trousers

There's some suggest
these annual baptisms
be shifted to a pond
on the barrens
made more hospitable
by three months of summer heat—
I say get behind me Satan,
the ocean is where God's sorrows
reside in the world
a wilderness to pierce
the heart of the lost
if they want comfort let them
join the Sally Ann

The penitents walk into the harbour
where Brother Harold
awaits them in tie and suspenders
and banker's spectacles
solemn as an executioner—
drowns each sinner
in the stinging cold
and they rise up shriven
aquiver with the Lord in their veins
forever and ever
amen

2.

you hears the Lord
when Mr. Scaines holds
your head beneath the water
that's what I was told,
a voice ringing from the other side
of the tide's mauzy drone

it's like a mother speaking aloud
while you're still part of her
Dorcas Pottle said,
before you come wholly
into the world of sin
before you're wholly alone

kept my eyes wide
while I was under
as if that would help me hear,
as if to let Jesus enter by
any door He might
but the ocean stopped my ears
or I was deafened by some fault
of my own
and lifted into the light
with neither word to carry

forsaken is how I felt—
fell against the hands at my side
wanting to fight,
wanting to be lowered back down

eyes burning out of my head
with the water's salt

3.

washed in the blood
of the lamb amen,
I wants a good dunking
right enough

brothers and sisters
I spent half me days
in drinking
and the other half
repenting of it—
like sculling out
to an empty trap
and home again,
all's to show for your trip
is blisters

bloody great shock
of the water every time,
so cold going under
it's like being shorn
front and back
with a rusty blade,
surprised there's no scars
to tell the scouring

only down a second
before Harold Scaines
hauls you out by the armpits
but I never felt so clean
as coming up into the glow
of those faces attending

on the landwash,
all praying for my sake

I been sove three times now

please God this one will take

CONFESSION

Newfoundland South Coast ca. 1900

it wasn't us was at it

whatever it is you're looking
to blame us for

we just come up now
from heaving rocks
at the gulls down on the point

the priest comes through one sunday a month
and shag all to do after mass
so we goes to flick a few rocks
no harm in it

pious there always got a rock in he's hand
but only for a game of pitch and toss
or to be throwing at the gulls

we baits a hook on a string sometimes
hauls them birds around
like a busted kite

jimmy's mother says
it's a sin to be at it
god's creatures too she tells him

father says only a woman
would worry about what happens
to them fucken old gulls

they're just rats with wings
is what he says

that's jimmy there
looking at he's shoes
to keep from bawling
got one on a hook today
and feeling bad about it now

got to wait a whole month
before he gets another chance
at confession

SMALL CLOTHES

near Corner Brook, Newfoundland ca. 1940

This is where he told me to stand
under the washing on the line

He'd come up the hill lugging his camera
and set it down in the garden,
staring out over the harbour with both hands
to the small of his back like he'd just bought
the place from God

Didn't see me there till I said hello,
him jumping and rubbing his palms together then,
like someone up to no good,
told me to stand over there,
never even asked after my name

I stood over there like he said
my dress billowing out with the washing
and I never felt so foolish

What do you want me to do I asked him
Look out at the water he said
I said What's to look at out there?
You just look he said

My mother said he was a queer stick
to take a picture and not even
ask me to smile for it

She was hiding in the kitchen all this time
and never come out first or last

Wouldn't be caught dead
talking to some man who'd seen
her small clothes faffering in the breeze

Sit down, my son, sit down, she won't stir now till dark. Gives me an hour's peace of an evening to smoke. Never had no use for cigarettes but I'd as soon take a pipe as a feed of salt beef. And you can tell by the look of me I don't mind eating.

She always said what she loved about me was my appetite, that I was an easy man to keep happy. I take that to mean she got nothing complimentary to say about my looks but I never held it against her. Ate whatever was put in front of me and fell into flesh. Sat with a pipe after supper to watch her clear the table and put the house to rights.

All that women's work and the looking out for her I does now, she won't abide anyone else in her kitchen so I learned to cook after a fashion. Spoons soup to her and washes her arms and legs with a warm cloth before we settles for the night. She keeps a hand to my belly while we lies there, pinches it like a youngster's cheek—proud of it she is, as if it was a prize creature she raised from a pup.

Her dirtiest days she'll say Hubert, some young thing will put the gaff on you before the first spade of gravel hits my casket. I tells her I got my doubts about that notion, a man can't help his face after all.

No, that's just a gull out the harbour you're after hearing, she's sound up there a while yet.

That's a lovely evening out there now, that is.

49

DEAD MAN'S POND

from the Carter Genealogy, Provincial Archives

Late of Ferryland, Robert Carter
was a Justice of the Peace.
Below the tide's mark of high water
he built a flake on Benger's Beach.

His son Robert wed Eliza
and she was laid to rest
the year they brought their hay
in from the meadow back of Pitts.

Catherine, wife of William,
lived to ninety-nine,
her ancient corpse set down between
Mrs. Carter and Miss Weston.

Black Bob passed suddenly,
he was owner of the Downs;
of his wife no word on when she
died or who lies next her in the ground.

Peter wed Sydney Livingston
before he was shot by Long.
Monier drowned, Charles died young,
Eliza's girl wed Woolcombe.

Long Bob sliced his knee
bathing in Freshwater River.
Kate went to Glory at seventy-three.
John will be eight years old forever.

Peter's grandson perished
in the depths of Deadman's Pond
trying to save two foolish
girls. Both girls also drowned.

Samuel never took a wife.
He died alone at the age of Christ.

CAUSE OF DEATH AND REMARKS

from Jerrett's Genealogy, Provincial Archives

Died suddenly. Died young.
Fell overboard and drowned.
Boat capsized while hunting loons,
body never found.

Lived one hour.
Lived with brother George.
Lost on schooner coming from St. John's
with all hands on board.

Jaundice. Senility. Apoplexy.
Died in First World War.
Died fishing on the Labrador.
Joined Salvation Army.

Tuberculosis. Influenza.
Multiple myeloma.
Must have died young,
not remembered by sister Julia.

Died of old age. Pleuritis.
Coronary thrombosis.
Operated Post Office
at Cavendish.

MARK WATERMAN, LIGHTKEEPER (RETIRED), ADDRESSES HIS SUCCESSOR CA. 1931

So this is Rag's Island,
she's yours now and welcome.

Thought I might have a few words
to hold you in good stead

some small bit of wisdom
but I'm starting to have me doubts.

Keep yourself occupied
or the place will mozzle your head

send you gabbling about
the cliffs after the birds.

My first winter I heard
voices adrift in the wind

sat awake for days on end
scribbling notes of what was said

before I come to my senses.
Go on and laugh, it sounds

like so much foolishness
to someone just come aboard.

All told the life's not that bad.
The Duty chart's a fair guide

of what the job asks of a man.
Drink as much as you can afford.

Any more I could think to add
you're too green to understand.

February and a savage night
to be out, wind eighty knots,

waves cresting fifty feet,
a body would last only minutes

adrift in that ocean
but we went looking regardless.

The lifeboat was red fibreglass,
white plastic tarp for a cabin,

now and again a light would flash
inside so you knew there was men

aboard, though in what condition
or how many you couldn't guess.

A second vessel worked close
enough to heave them a line

and we counted eight or nine
in lifejackets over street clothes,

more again huddled at the back.
Lost sight of them in a trough

just as they tipped into the bleak
and the men pitched from the raft—

we come over the wave's peak
and those life-vest locator

lights were like stars on the water.
Didn't have the heart to figure

numbers against the black
but we were close enough to hear

them calling and pretended
we might manage a rescue still,

flinging our boat hooks from the rail
as if our own lives depended

on the show. You had to try it
even so you knew how things ended.

Carried on a long while
after the last of them went quiet.

He was the last keeper at Cape St. Mary's before the light was automated. His people all from Red Head Cove and he once had the burnished copper hair to prove it. Not much above a youngster when he tended his first light on Baccalieu, just him and the wife out there, women and their ways another remote island he'd chosen to strand himself on. A privacy he was learning to love the strangeness of. The first child born to them in a storm and when Agnes told him to cut the cord he snipped too near the navel to knot it, had to tie the umbilicus off with a shoelace. Family the only company they had most of their lives together, keeping one isolated lighthouse after another along the coast. Carried that shoelace in a pocket all his days.

There was an empty keeper's house next his own at the Cape where birders camped out in latter years, scientists and students and eccentrics drawn by the migratory colonies on the cliffs. Two or three burrowing in for the season, scores arriving for weekend counts under the weight of binoculars and field guides and forty-ouncers. He drank the nights dry in their company, laughter loose in his chest, carcinogenic, a flooded engine turning over. His light endlessly stirring the darkness out over the water. Agnes rocking sober and silent in a corner as the room pitched on its ear, slipping off to bed unnoticed in the racket.

When the guitar made its rounds Vince would pass it off shyly. He'd demur a second time without touching the instrument, like a man refusing a drink too tempting to look upon. Third time round he cradled and kept it, trawling through a repertoire of folk songs and shanties, old country tunes fished from the background static on a lonely radio. He had one eyetooth missing, a gap where he'd snug his cigarette butt so he could play and smoke and sing at the one time. Never slept until all hands were down and maybe it was the years spent in small company he was making up for. Drank preserving alcohol one night when the songs outlasted the booze, cups of ethanol meant for pickling specimens passed around, the stink of it cut with coca cola. Never so in all my life, sir. Hey diddle-diddle-die, diddle-die-doe.

And up the double-helix staircase spiralling the walls of the tower next morning, polishing the flash of mirrors and brass to a sheen.

Talk always comes round to Vince when the birders gather at the Cape. How he strung a rope thick as a man's wrist from his back door to the tower to lead him blind through the fog and the black, clung to it in wind that could strip the shoes from your feet. How a storm surge once doused the light with granite stones thrown a hundred yards up the cliff-face, Vince gathering scattered shards of the prism for months afterward, passing them to friends as a keepsake.

They stumble through his favourite songs, the tight knots he made of them coming loose in their mouths, verses out of order, lines misplaced or forgotten. Fall back on the language of field notes finally, as if comparing sightings of some rare creature glimpsed seasons ago. Bald crown of the head mantled with white tufts, tawny median stripe of nicotine staining the snowy beard. The one missing eyetooth. That gap.

UNDER
SILK

Out of Toronto en route to New Delhi,
24 hours from a hotel room's strange
familiar where we'll lie, addled by
jetlag and the season's upended light,
and feeling almost at home there,
being naked and next one another.
At the lip of the Atlantic's western range
our vapour trail chalks the domestic blues
above Red Indian Lake, the Exploits
River furrowing an ocean of spruce,
the mine's tapped-out ore shafts jigsawed
beneath pre-fab residential streets,
every intricately detailed room
from the dollhouse of my childhood.

What a journey it was trekking through town
on winter afternoons, hauling a toboggan
past the hockey rink and Royal Stores
to the sliding hills behind the Union
Hall; our lakeside cabin a distant moon
to the company house where my brothers
and I slept two to a bed. Across the bog and
tailings pond, the mill's high windows loomed
like the lights of some great ship moored
with engines idling, its latent motion
a quiver ringing through the floorboard.

That town was my first love, profound
and partial and easy enough to betray
with the suspicion important things lay
elsewhere, a hunch kept under the mattress
and thumbed through in my dreams, a compulsive tic,
the tremor of an adult world so exotic
and unlikely one day's travel conjures sleepless
India and a foreign bed in Delhi,
you lying naked there beside me.

HOPE CHEST

Something Old

Shale foundation and a drainpipe's dead
stump dwarfed by seedling pine and alder
rising through the ghost of floorboard

and swept canvas. A concrete step where
the backdoor once opened onto Nan's yard
still overlooked by the lilac that held her

dark-panelled hallway in shades of shade
all summer; laden with blossoms each June,
branches swaying into waist-high grass

under the weight of a sweetness
too flagrant to last. Might have considered
the same true of us when we began,

lavish haze flowering from every gesture,
the kind of extravagance that can floor
the senses and keeps less than a season,

but the world will make a stranger
of the most obvious expectation.
Couldn't have guessed, those childhood

vacations I slept in an upstairs room,
that what seemed most sound and certain
about the property would disappear

and the lilac endure in its absence,
spilling out over the ancient fence,
palings foundering beneath the bloom.

Something New

When test results confirmed what we feared
Dad was moved to the terminal ward

and my mother rarely left his side,
all day to help him to and from his bed,

to wash and feed him, rub his calves
and feet, and she stayed there half

the nights as well, wouldn't give in to sleep,
sat up in a chair so she could keep

tabs on any sound or motion from
her husband lying across the room.

Her nights at home I stayed with Dad
but once he'd taken his evening meds

I slept through till morning unless he called.
Weeks into that shiftwork before he told

me the sleeping pills leached clear
of his system in the loneliest hours

and he lay quiet at three and four
so as not to disturb his company,

dead to the world on a cot near the floor.
I could never match Mom's fidelity

to the vigil, admired it from a distance
that seemed a lack in me, a resistance

I've always felt to risking love,
the cut of it that goes hand in glove

with tying yourself to something as frail
as another person. Bound to fail

was my thought and I always managed
to keep well clear, but my parents' marriage

in its final days on the cancer ward
made me think I'd lived my life a coward.

Not the most romantic lines
to preface a wedding declaration

but I don't know how else to name
the place I started from, to frame

how new this is, believing we're equal
to what the world might offer or steal

from us in the time we're given.
We're not young enough to ask for heaven

on earth, but here's a promise I will make—
to stay by you, to be fully awake.

Something Borrowed

An apple you left on my desk
a month ago or longer—
bruises dimple the crown,
but the red circumference
is still as firm as a fist.

Every day I shift it among
books and receipts, shopping lists,
like a subway passenger
half asleep underground,
shunted station to station.

Always I lift and set it down
carefully by the stem.
Can just resist the temptation
to lick your fingerprints
off its nearly flawless skin.

Something Blues

You better come on in my kitchen,
cause it's going to be raining outdoors
　　　　—Robert Johnson

Almost quit before I met you,
didn't sit up nights by the phone,
I was halfways gone to believing
I'd be better off on my own,
I came on in a few kitchens
and hummed a few bars of that song—
it wasn't love, it just kept me busy
until you came along.

I've driven this block a time or two
but I never gave up the keys,
always kept one foot out the door
so I could hightail it when I pleased,
I came on in a few kitchens
where everything right went wrong—
it wasn't love, it just kept me busy
until you came along.

[bridge]
Didn't know it was you I was missing
when I went out on the town,
tried to tell myself I was serious
when I was just messing around,
fell into some cool clear water
but it never ran deep enough,
Lord, it was something,
but it wasn't love.

Almost quit before I met you,
didn't sit up nights by the phone,
I was halfways gone to believing
I'd be better off on my own,
I came on in a few kitchens
but I never stayed in there long—
it wasn't love, it just kept me busy
until you came along.

Their hands are busy defacing the world as
you sleep, altering your place in their lives
one detail at a time—you barely recognize
the bedroom come morning, furniture
shifted, picture frames monkeyed askew.
They leave all the doors of your head ajar,
purr over the branching tributaries
of your confusion like 16th-century explorers
fingering a map of terra incognito,
convinced they're making you up as they go.
They flick on the lamps of your childhood
to make you feel naked in your clothes,
vital organs backlit and sitting like food
on a tray they can prod for any sign
of blight—*Does that hurt? Is that sore?*
Twice a month Canada Post delivers
a moment of clarity and terror in a plain
white envelope, a note in your own hand
that says the kids are alright, but you'll never
forgive them for making you feel so human.
Turn out their pockets before you throw
the day's laundry in the washing machine
on the off chance you might discover
the glassy marble of your heart among
the lint, hard and polished and just small
enough to swallow whole.

Unplug the insatiable telephone,
the apocalypse unfolding hourly
on the network news crawl.

Ignore the kitchen's Victorian factory
of filthy dishes, the laundry pile
suffocating a lost child in the basement.

Ignore the lost children.
Forget music and saffron and oysters,
put aside the clichéd, the quaint

rituals of wine and lingerie—
aphrodisiacs are for amateurs
with more time than common sense,

who've yet to learn bliss is stolen
from the world in small, piercing slivers.
Think of stealth as foreplay

in the prison yard of daily events,
sneak out of your clothes
as soon as the coast is clear—

the air raid siren of a youngster
crying is about to rise
through the bedroom floor,

the weight of the Three Gorges reservoir
has altered the planet's rotation
by the same rate at which yesterday's

dishes are going septic in the sink—
be resolute. Bliss lives for bliss alone,
apply yourself to that ephemeral sliver.

You have less time than you think.

PUB CRAWL IN DUBLIN

Full moon above O'Connell
as we drain pints in a row
of ancient pubs featuring a press

at the bar and the same football
highlight reel and a tiled loo
down a sheer staircase

that gets steeper as we go,
the lunar eclipse underway
adding a note of gravity

to the evening's excess,
another brimming Guinness
in another shabby taproom

for each pale fingernail
of light clipped by darkness.
My wife's first trip to Dublin

and all night we circle
a nameless brother stillborn
and buried anonymous

in an angel's grave while
her father studied medicine
here half a century past—

can't help imagining him
with us, a spectral third wheel
on our erratic wander,

though the crawl wasn't planned
as tribute or memorial
and the child isn't mentioned

as the eclipse nears full term,
as Holly flirts with two Swiss
students in her nascent German,

as we join a drunken local
on a maundering version of "Sam Hall" —
by the time we surrender

our empties near the Grand Canal
the world is our tavern
and genial publican,

the absent moon's silver rim
like the base of a pint glass
drawn and set on the bar,

a nightcap for the stroll
across the bridge to our hotel,
and what all evening I guessed

was grief shadowing her face
seems more a kind of wonder
to be here and alive at all,

to have her brother close at last.

Your naked back when my eyes slur
open, prostrate in some hotel,
high windows amping the sun's glare,
light like a wire brush on skin—

last night's lunar eclipse blurs
through the steady drizzle
of feedback, and the reprimand
we earned for singing "Sam Hall"

with too much native emotion—
no regrets but the headache
and even that the dead would envy
if there was your heat to lean

into as salve against the static,
how many verses did we crucify
before the bartender intervened
to say he'd had enough?

Passed a poet cast in bronze
on a bench beside the waterway
as we crossed the Grand Canal,
pretending to pay us no mind,

as if he was content with the swans
of his make-believe afterlife—
didn't turn a hair when the moon
went black and we staggered through

his darkened corner of heaven
but I expect Patrick Kavanagh
(1904 – 1967)
won't forget us anytime soon.

VAMPIRES, ETC.

She wants to know if I've been eating garlic.
This after a kiss I stopped to offer
at the door, on my way to pick

up a carload of Halloween candy.
No malice intended that I can see,
in fact it's the kind of question

that seems overdue, eight years in.
On the lawn a counterfeit cemetery,
headstones for the faux-deceased.

Ate a full clove, I tell her,
to keep the vampires in check,
and this seems a satisfactory answer.

For the moment at least.

DAHLIAS

We drove downtown to hear an African band
at the Ship, the dahlia bulbs you'd brought
for the flowerbed fronting my house briefly
forgotten, drowsing in their newspaper shells on
the back seat while we planted ourselves near
the speakers, the music migrant and unfamiliar
and meant for dancing, an all-white crowd
working hard to meet the music's expectations.

I was in a dancing phase when we met, as if
I'd just discovered beauty in life and was willing
to look foolish for a glimpse of its taillights,
to travel awhile in beauty's wake—
my box garden on the sidewalk rooted in
the same impulse, coddling green, learning
the names of flowers to coax them into
the world and myself along for the ride,
planting your dahlias by the light through
my front window at 3 a.m., the bulbs already
nursing shoots in the shade of last fall's news.

This was months before we fell in love,
when we could only feel the furl of it
gathering, but there was no impatience
in us, just that hard kernel biding its time.
I was happy to stand in the dark under stars
as you drove away, the red bloom at
the foot of the street when you braked
to turn the corner, a foreign music at work
in my life that I was willing to look a fool

in courting. Those dahlias never did flower
and we joked about it all summer,
that's how certain we were.

UNDER SILK

1.
My wife is dead, is dead, is dead
and I'm crawling a cold hardwood
hallway bawling to beat the band
when I come to myself in bed,
darkened room rising piecemeal
to a grey light: bookcase, nightstand,
the duvet cover we purchased
while passing through Rajasthan,
Holly under silk beside me,
her breath a calm surf that dresses
and undresses its stretch of sand,
and I'm struck by the strangeness
in that inscrutable syllable
wife, its veiled etymology,
that medieval stone fortress
moated and wreathed in mist—
whisper the word like a spell
from a cryptic German fable,
picking at the dream's surface
as if its details were a scab grown
over a truth more elusive,
the widowed hunchback all the while
keening like some inconsolable
ancient on a forsaken beach,
full fathoms beyond the solace
of language, of human speech.

2.

We'd strolled down into Jodhpur
from the heights of a fairytale
castle where successive Moghuls
layered their filigreed courts one
on another like sediment
settling in elaborate moulds,
each set of narrow marble stairs
a portal between the ages,
as if to teach time's long lesson
in the space of an afternoon.
Dusk before we found the merchant
near the market's clock tower,
eight ramshackle flights honeycombed
with the incongruous splendour
of pashmina and cotton,
of handwoven carpets and shawls
displayed by a fey, shoeless salesman
who parachuted his wares'
raw silk and organza at our feet,
so much beauty it seemed unfair
we could have it for so little,
each item settling to the floor
with the stiff, textured rustle
of wet paper dried in sunlight,
and we leafed through them like pages
recovered from an ocean current,
the fugitive words lost to sight
but still faintly, faintly there.

THE
LANDING

A CARRY-ON

You'll want to pack a toothbrush,
a good book, your razor.

A lengthy skein of wool, a flash-
light and extra batteries,

cigarettes to curry favour
with the shades and wraiths,

to trade for tips, directions.
Songs for the broken-hearted

uploaded to your iPod,
pictures of the dearly departed

to identify their blank eyes
among the astonishing press of the dead.

Nothing you can't afford
to leave behind or lose.

A list of yes-or-no questions
you'd like to have answered.

A second pair of sensible shoes.

OFF-STAGE

He wasn't gone a month when I saw him
alive and well the first time, on a low cot
in a labyrinthine hospital basement,
left sleeve rolled high as if he'd just donated
a pint of blood, his right hand rising to
greet me like a doll's arm craned at
the elbow by an off-stage puppeteer.
Knew before waking it was a dream of
my father in the quick, a shadow cast by
the mind, though his half-smile suggested
our meeting was as much a surprise to him,
that I was the unexpected apparition
in his solitary afterlife.

My parents' retirement home in St. John's,
Dad a young man with hands kitty-corner on
kitchen counters, conducting a patient
interrogation of my childhood self after
an attempt to kill my older brother in a fist fight.
I guess I miss you the only explanation
that murderous alter ego could muster
and the dream's jerry-rigged works suddenly
showed through the surface gloss,
loneliness and grief playing dress-up
behind the curtained subconscious.

Those sporadic visitations spanned a year
or two, sly nods from the apocryphal beyond,
a temporary salve that burned even
as it helped close the cut—

there was never an instance in those encounters
when my father and I touched,
impossible to say if that reticence
was his or mine alone.

DEADFALL

At the old farm garden with John Fitzgerald,
sunlight in the copse of trees filtered green

and liquid as light through an aquarium,
beams of birch and spruce brought down

by wind and going to rot where they fell—
it gives the droke the feel of a building

abandoned and falling into ruin
at the edge of a derelict field

overgrown with wild rose and bramble.
Stand clear when Johnny wields

the chainsaw, pintailing chips and bark
like sparks showering off a welding

torch as he limbs out the deadfall
and skins the punky rind from

lengths still solid enough to burn.
My job is to drag the logs he's milled

to a quad and four-post trailer parked
where bush encroaches on the garden,

to clear the sheared scrag in his wake,
to suggest likely candidates among

the sticks of firewood composting
on forest floor or caught up in

the hammock of neighbouring branches,
though it's hard to guess what we can take

by looking, the rot flares at the core
and smoulders outward ring by ring.

Tempted to make something more
of that detail squatting on its haunches

in the underwater light as we work
but John would only shake his head

at the conceits I entertain on the side.
My job is hauling and stacking wood.

It's simple waste he can't abide.

THE GANGES, AT MIDDLE AGE

They stopped on the walkway
below my living room window,

spent fifteen minutes making out
on concrete steps in the dark

oblivious to the cold and wet,
pausing occasionally to check

the time, talking together in low
voices about god knows what,

love or ontology or a curfew
they were wearing at the fringes.

Can't recall what woke me
or why I left my bed to brood

here in the gloom, insomniac,
some creaky hinge of middle age,

the kind of worry that changes
nothing, makes us voyeurs

of our own lame circumstances,
the roof maybe, the mortgage,

the uneasy sense of drift and decay
that dogs the night's smallest hours.

Heard them before I could pick
any detail clear of shadow

and not much surfaced through the murk,
couldn't see where hands were busy

or what buttons were undone,
but the physical intimacy

was raw, almost pornographic,
they might have been eating food

off each others' naked skin—
felt like a dirty old prick

spying on the private ceremony
but couldn't make myself look away.

I watched those anonymous pilgrims dive
into the foul water of the Ganges

as if touched by something holy
a moment that went on for ages,

blissful both, arrayed with flowers,
before meandering downstream slowly

toward the lights on Highland Drive.

THE LANDING

Ten years he's been dead when I find my
self engaged in some extracurricular
with two girls who seem, on the face of things,
not quite old enough to buy their own liquor.

The slight brunette saunters off to powder
her nose, adorned only in pearl earrings,
but she hesitates at the door, spooked by
the knell of footsteps ringing up the stair,

and I'm ushered out to meet the intruder—
my father, circa his days at the mill,
shapeless work shirt, a wisp of thinning hair,
the walrus moustache still black as coal.

"It's my Dad," I tell the girls and stare
as the deliberate figure comes to rest
shy of the landing on the top floor,
his dark eyes glassy and expressionless.

"It's just a dream," I announce to no one,
alone with him now and wanting free
of whatever compulsion conjured the man,
grief or bald shame or some muddier charm

delivering that absence within one arm
length, one step down the ancient stairway.
Our lives are simpler than we care to see.
Even in the thorniest circumstance,

we dismiss the heart as a mystery
to avoid ourselves or, worse, put make-up
on a pig, to use my father's term.
He lingers there in a familiar silence,

never much for reprimand or handing
out advice, but he seems not to know his own
flesh and when I step off the landing
to reach for him, of course, I wake up.

QUESTIONS OF TRAVEL

...the choice is never wide and never free.
                    —Elizabeth Bishop

After her mother lost her mind
she was shunted among family
in Nova Scotia and New England,

a little wandering heirloom,
a great-uncle's postcard painting
no one could bear to throw away,

hanging awhile in a back room
before being consigned
to some relative's steamer trunk.

In college she turned to poetry,
then to wanderlust and drink,
but as a child there was no respite

and she rebelled by making herself ill
with asthma and constipation,
with spells of vertigo or fainting,

her protest passive and internal—
tucked her head under sheets at night,
the only soul awake in Worcester

as she signalled SOS with a flashlight,
and that early miniature
managed to contain

every landscape yet to come.
She grew up a curious creature,
writing as if she were certain

that something out there loves us all
but never completely at home
in the world, never married

for long to a single place or person —
she travelled to escape the fear
she was her mother's daughter,

to have something useful
to do with the baggage she carried,
to keep her buried head above water.

A STONE

When her husband died she placed a gravestone
with her name and birthdate next his own,

a blank left to mark the day she'd be gone
from the world, took each morning on loan

and managed twenty years with afternoon
soaps, *Wheel of Fortune*, the rotary phone.

That empty space like a Buddhist koan,
the sound of one hand clapping, something sewn

into a coat's lining and forgotten
in a basement closet, a rock she'd thrown

so hard and high she couldn't have known
where or when it might come down.

That shrouded date was the Lord's dominion
and she wore it like an invisible crown.

A KEEPSAKE

My father passed in his hospital bed
after a hellish fall of wasting flesh

and I leaned in to kiss his alien face
before leaving him to the dead,

the familiar smell when my lips brushed
his temple like a garden bloom,

the light of every cell extinguished
and that one human vestige abiding,

a keepsake I pocketed and carried home
to press between the pages of a book.

Months go by these days before I think
of it, dormant on a shelf in my office,

and even then I approach it sidelong,
staying downwind so as not to spook

the skittish memory, choosing random
spines and browsing, aimless and intent,

so I might happen on it as if by accident,
a last trace of my father startled from ink

and paper, singular and undiminished,
before it shies from the light, slips back

into the shade of endless forest.

There was someone up the shore had a new Brownie camera
and Nan sent along a message asking him down, to have their
pictures drawn off. It might have been someone named Moore
or Mercer, Aunt Helen says. Not anyone they knew well.

It's their Sunday best they have on, mid-morning, before
they walk up through Riverhead to the church. Clustered like
berries on a bush, heads bare to the cold but for the salt &
pepper cap my grandfather wears. Their shadows cast sidelong
into a stand of firewood curing against the shed. Uncle
Clyde's hand-me-down jacket two sizes too small, already the
pinched look of a school-teacher about him. Dad's hands like a
lace collar on his little sister's shoulders, white against her
black coat, his thumbs tucked under her chin. A face only a
mother could love, Aunt Helen always said, and she's scowling
at the man ordering them around their own yard, telling them
where to stand.

It was a camera you held at waist-height, the Brownie. The
photographer framing them in the viewfinder, head bowed as
if waiting for the minister's benediction at church. As if
looking into a well, telling the upturned faces to hold still
before the shutter clicked.

This is the year before my grandfather died. Nan is holding
Dad's arm, standing a little to his side. Her son, at fifteen,
half a foot taller than her husband. The dinner vegetables
already peeled, waiting to go on the stove, Nan's apron hung
on the pantry door when they called her outside. A scuff of
snow on her indoor shoes.

They'll be off to church now the once in their overcoats
and galoshes, salt beef and cabbage on the boil. Their

likenesses caught on a strip of film, those faces innocent of what the years hold in store. Aunt Helen the last in that picture still living, the old house torn down, the yard overgrown with wild roses and pine trees and alder.

None of them could have imagined me here, trying to read their expressions as they stand endlessly at attention, in that moment before the future is set alight. To their eyes I'm just another stranger on the far side of the camera, head bowed as if expecting some sort of blessing. Wanting them to hold still. For some reason the stranger wants that more than anything and he keeps repeating it under his breath. Hold still, he says, for the love of God.

Hold still.

BURN BARREL

Halfway out the yard
an ancient barrel once
used as incinerator
for scrap wood and garden
waste, its face obscured
by a skirt of spent grass
and raspberry canes.
The teacher who scarred
my father's youth
with math and grammar
and Alfred, Lord Tennyson
lived somewhere in the pasture
beyond the back fence,
though the house is long gone,
passed into oblivion
as if fed board by board
to the barrel's mouth.
Dad could still recite
those Victorian verses
his last months alive
and there seems some truth
in that, half-realized,
a lesson whose little light
blooms and dies back each season
and can't be seen entire,
though it was just a party trick
in my father's eyes.
Behind the grassy screen
the barrel is so thick
with rust it's porous,

eaten through by salt air
and by something kin
to its own blind appetite—
time's slow, smokeless fire.

THE STARS, AFTER JOHN'S HOMEBREW

He carts them up from the basement
two at a time, empties each green bottle

into a measuring cup, slow-pours your glass
to siphon off the gravelly sediment.

Bitter fizz in the nose that doesn't last,
a gnarly blend of sour green apple

and sugar, a finish that would throttle
the song of a hermit thrush.

"Another drop of the WD-70?"
he asks halfway through your first

when one is more than plenty—
the second a patch of stinging nettle

with a briny gasoline undertone
and the subtlest hint of immortality,

the third enough to plant you face down
among the spuds in Johnny's garden.

May as well have another this far in,
his wife won't let you chance the car

even after you sober up a little
on a lunch of molasses bread and tea,

you'll have to stagger around the harbour
with the ocean's sweet nothing in your ears,

and the stars, lord jesus, the stars!
the grit of sediment beginning to settle

in night's enormous still, their thorny glare
rattling the dark like a length of sheet-metal.

DISSENTING OPINIONS

Jared Bland at House of Anansi. Stan Dragland at 113 Bond. John Barton et al on the opposite coast. Holly Hogan on Connemara Place.

PREVIOUS APPEARANCES

Arc, The Malahat Review, The March Hare Anthology, The New Quarterly, The Newfoundland Quarterly, Riddle Fence, Toronto Poetry Vendors.

The pieces in "Dead Man's Pond" were written for *Intangible Evidence* at The Rooms in St. John's, an exhibit conceived and curated by Shauna McCabe. Thanks to the staff at the Provincial Archives for humouring me.

"Viewfinder" and "Something New" were featured in the NFB documentary *Hard Light,* a 2011 film by Justin Simms.

RANDOM THANKS

Sapporo. Francois. The Canada Council. Coffee & Co. Annette Clarke. Woody Point. Health Sciences Centre nurses. The White Hills. Salt beef. The Duke of Duckworth. Woollen vamps. *The Great Fires.* Hospitality suites. The Smiths. Potatoes. The Piper's Frith. Baccalieu Island. Vitamin D. Mark Ferguson. Sidecars. *The Goldberg Variations.* John and Mary Fitzgerald. "C. C. Rider." The Tely 10. "Carrying someone else's infant past a cow in a field near Marmora, Ont." The Spur (RIP). Wasabi. India. Michael Winter's yellow dory. WAM. Kim Jernigan. Rhubarb jam. Folk Night at The Ship. Ginger Gravol. MKF. *Hejira.* Holly's small things. Every last one.

Photo: Andrew MacCormack

Michael Crummey is the author of four books of poetry, and a book of short stories, *Flesh and Blood*. His first novel, *River Thieves*, was a finalist for the Scotiabank Giller Prize, and his second, *The Wreckage*, was a national bestseller and a finalist for the Rogers Writers' Trust Fiction Prize. His most recent novel, the bestselling *Galore*, won the Commonwealth Writers' Prize for Best Book. *Under the Keel* is his first collection in a decade. He lives in St. John's, Newfoundland.